101 WAYS TO HELP YOUR CHILD LEARN TO READ AND WRITE

BY

MARY AND RICHARD BEHM

New Learning
Concepts, Inc.

Educational Publishers

New Learning Concepts, Inc.
Educational Publishers
P.O. Box 7886
Bloomington, Indiana 47407

To order this book or other fine parent
involvement materials call 800-925-7853.

Book design: Kathleen McConahay
Cover design: David J. Smith
Cover photograph: R. Heinzen/Superstock
All interior photographs by David J. Smith, except those
on pages 2, 6, 20 (top), and 36 by CLEO.

Library of Congress Cataloging-in-Publication Data

Behm, Mary, 1956-
    101 ways to help your child learn to read and write / by
Mary and Richard Behm.
        p. cm.
    Rev. ed. of: 101 ideas to help your child learn to read and
write. c 1989
    Includes bibliographical references.
    ISBN 1–883790–16–6 (softcover)
    1. Children—Language—Handbooks, manuals, etc.
2. Language arts—Handbooks, manuals, etc. 3. Reading—
Language experience approach—Handbooks, manuals, etc.
4. Reading—Parent participation—Handbooks, manuals, etc.
5. Children—Books and reading—Handbooks, manuals, etc.
6. Children—Writing—Handbooks, manuals, etc. 7. Educational games—Handbooks, manuals, etc. 8. Parent and child—
Handbooks, manuals, etc. I. Behm, Richard, 1948- . II. Behm,
Mary, 1956- 101 ideas to help your child learn to read and
write. III. Title.
LB1139.L3B43 1995
649'.68—dc20   95-18220
                                       CIP

Table of Contents

You are your child's first and best teacher.

Dear Parents,

Learning to read and write starts at home, not in school. "You are your child's first and best teacher," affirm Richard and Mary Behm, the authors of these 101 ideas.

Parents, the home, the neighborhood—these are the first and most important teachers of literacy. They show the child that reading and writing are real-world events, that reading and writing make life more interesting and enjoyable.

What sets this book apart from other books of fun-to-do things is its consistent emphasis on parents as initiators of literacy. Throughout your child's years at home and in school, you serve as a model. Your example forms an attitude in your child that encourages or discourages the use of language as a natural and fun way to learn.

The activities in this book do not require you to teach reading and writing in any formal way. These ideas remind you that you have informal opportunities to encourage your child's learning from the cradle through high school and to build a positive attitude toward learning through reading and writing. These activities are organized to fit the way we parents tend to think about our time with our children:

- in the nursery
- at bedtime
- on the road
- watching television

These activities also remind us to interact with our children in the way we ourselves want to be treated, as capable people with our own feelings and ideas. We do that through words of praise, through questions about opinions, through learning together.

This book is special because it offers you educationally sound ideas to promote reading and writing, but more especially because it encourages you to use reading and writing opportunities to build a warm relationship with your child.

Carl B. Smith, Ph.D.
Family Literacy Center
ERIC Clearinghouse on Reading,
English, and Communication

❦

How to Get Started

As both parents and teachers, we have come to see that one of the most important elements in a child's learning to read and write is a supportive home environment. Without a home in which language—speaking, listening, writing, and reading—is valued, success both in school and later life may be difficult. We have put together this book to help you help your child acquire skill in reading and writing. Perhaps more importantly, through the activities in this book, you and your child can form a closer, stronger relationship. Your child will gain not only skill but also lifelong pleasure in reading and writing, and you will gain your child's affection and respect. We base these activities on five principal ideas:

Play Is the Essence of Learning

This past summer we had a particularly large and very playful brood of chipmunks in our backyard. Their entertaining playfulness,

as is the case with all animals, served a serious end. So it is with human beings. Play involves us fully, and we learn most effectively through play. Think, for instance, of your child learning to talk or walk. You and your child made it a game, a kind of play. The two of you delighted in each gurgling sound and laughed at each wobbly step. So, too, the activities in this book are designed to make learning to read and write a natural event, one in which play is the guiding principle.

Speaking, Listening, Reading, and Writing Are Related

Many of the activities in this book use oral language activities as the basis for reading and writing. Research in this area tells us that strong oral language skills are necessary for most children to develop as readers and writers. Frequently, you'll find that the activities involve both writing and reading and also incorporate listening. Writing stories, reading stories, listening to stories, and telling stories—these actions are interrelated and reinforce each other.

Learning Brings the Family Together

Moments shared through the activities in this book will draw your family together. Since all of the activities involve both you and your child, they help foster a close, caring relationship. Many of today's parents hold jobs outside the home, while at the same time trying to be "full-time parents"; and there are many single-parent families. In these circumstances, time and energy for extensive projects simply are not available. We have therefore designed most of these activities so that they can be done in short periods of time—many of them take only a few minutes. Some can be done while you are busy with another task, such as preparing a meal; others are especially designed for working parents who must travel frequently.

Home Is the Center for Learning

You are your child's first and best teacher. When you show your child that reading, speaking, writing, and listening are valued in your home, you send him or her an important message. When you make reading and writing a part of nurturing, your child will view them with pleasure. When you tell your child stories from your own family history, life, and imagination, you reveal yourself to her or him and give your child "roots." Just as importantly, when you listen attentively to what your child has to tell, you are breeding a healthy ego and raising a confident, self-reliant person. Strong support for literacy in your home will insure that your child gets the most out of formal schooling.

Praise Fosters Growth

Reading and writing are admittedly difficult skills for many children to master. One of the most important things you can do is to provide bushels of praise. Just as when your child learns to walk or talk, the mastery of reading and writing requires your encouragement and emotional support.

Don't be overly concerned about correctness. When a child colors in a coloring book, there is no need to "stay within the lines." Similarly, when your child writes, neatness and correct spelling are less important than the joy and action of writing. We advocate "invented" spelling as your child struggles to learn to write. Let the child spell the words as best he or she can. Similarly, when your child reads aloud, don't worry if a few words get missed or mispronounced.

What is important is that you share, praise, and be a model. Sharing these 101 activities will pay off by helping your child learn to read and write, speak and listen; and it will foster a strong, close relationship between you and your child.

[A note about gender: Sometimes we write "he," sometimes we write "she." This seems preferable to "s/he" or "he or she." You may change the gender of the pronouns to suit your child.]

Mary and Richard Behm

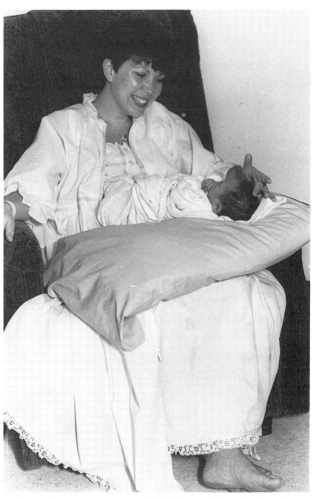

From the moment your child is born, learning begins.

In the Nursery

Researchers are finally discovering what many parents have known for years: From the moment your child was born, learning began. In this section you will find activities you can do to help stimulate that learning, to take advantage of your baby's growing fascination with language. During the nursery months, you can lay an important foundation for the later development of reading and writing skills.

1. Talk to Your Baby

Don't worry that she doesn't understand what you are talking about. She will associate your voice and the language you speak with the comfort and care you provide her. Don't be afraid to chatter away about what you are doing, whether you're driving a car, cleaning a room, or doing the office work you had to bring home with you. Hearing you talk will encourage your child to experiment with sounds; this experimentation will help your child develop the oral language necessary for other language skills.

2. Cooing

When your baby starts to coo, go ahead and coo back, repeating the sounds he is making. This may very well be your baby's first experience with the power of language: *He's* making *you* make noise.

3. Imitation

Repeat words and phrases often, letting your baby see your face. Soon you will notice your baby trying to imitate your sounds. Praise with a smile or a hug, and keep at it!

4. Indulge Yourself

Hold, kiss, caress, play pat-a-cake and "This Little Piggy." Physical stimulation is important for your child's learning. Psychologists and sociologists assure us that holding your baby will *not* spoil him. When a child cries, usually something is wrong—a wet diaper, a hungry feeling, or just loneliness. You would not enjoy being left alone in a dark room to cry yourself to sleep, and neither does your child.

5. Pretty Pictures

Just as physical stimulation is important, so also is visual stimulation. Mobiles above the crib, attractive pictures in the nursery, and putting your baby where she can see what's going on around her—all of these things keep her eyes filled with color and beauty, and her mind active and alert.

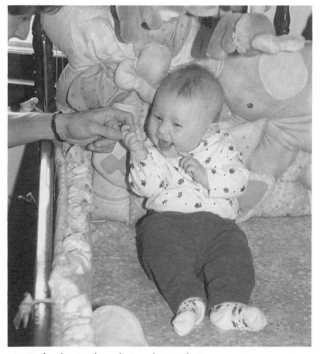

Both physical and visual stimulation are important.

6. First Stories

Begin reading stories to your baby as soon as you can. He won't understand the story, but he will be fascinated with the sound of the words. He will also grow up associating books with warm, pleasant times. A bonus: Bedtime stories that become a nightly ritual in the nursery make bedtime easier as your baby becomes a toddler.

7. Reading Habits

All language is interesting to your baby. When you're reading the newspaper or a recipe or a novel, read some of it aloud. A fussy baby will often quiet at the sound of your voice, and as she grows, your baby will want to imitate your reading habits. It's not unusual to discover a toddler sitting in a chair with an open book—upside down perhaps—but obviously wanting to be reading, just like Mom and Dad.

8. Sing to Your Baby

Most of us can carry a tune, at least a little, and your baby won't mind if you hit a few flat notes or can't remember all the words. In fact, you can make up your own nonsense song about an animal or hum your own lullaby. Find a couple of single lines and an easy melody, and you're all set. You might even want to write the words down to give to your child when he is older.

9. The Name Game

Get in the habit of saying the names of objects that you use around your baby. For example, if you bottle-feed your baby, say "bottle" each time you feed your baby. She'll begin to associate the sound of that word with the object, and you may soon find her attempting to imitate the sound of the word. Also, talk with your child about her toys and stuffed animals, giving them names: Teddy, Dolly, Doggie, etc.

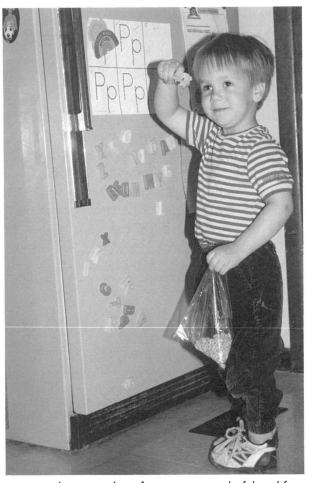

Magnetic letters on the refrigerator are colorful and fun.

❦

Around the Home

Your home is filled with opportunities to develop your child's reading and writing skills. The possibilities are nearly endless. In this section we present some activities you can use at home. Many of the activities are brief, but they could be extended if time permits. With a little effort, you can certainly devise numerous other activities on your own.

10. Author! Author!

Books written and illustrated by your child make treasured gifts to grandpas and grandmas, aunts and uncles. For the very young child, offer to print or type the story while she dictates. Take this masterwork to your local photocopy machine and make inexpensive copies of your child's book. If there is no copy store near you, post offices, libraries, and sometimes even supermarkets have copy machines available for public use. Authors love to get their works published: Your child will derive a reinforcing sense of achievement from "getting published."

11. Drawing and Writing

As soon as they can hold a crayon, children love to draw pictures and try to make letters. Encourage your toddler to give a title to her picture, and help her trace the letters of the title onto her drawing. Then post her drawing: Artists love to have their own show. (Here's another use for those magnetic letters—it will probably be years before you see the surface of your refrigerator again!)

12. Cooking to Read

Many children love to "help" with the cooking—especially if you're baking cookies. If your child is on a stool beside you, read your recipe out loud as you go along, letting your child add ingredients or help with stirring. As your child grows, let him read the directions— as much as he can. This helps make the connection between the practical and the pleasurable side of reading. A bonus: You will be helping your child become familiar with measuring cups and spoons, perhaps making fractions easier later on. Also, you'll be teaching him to cook.

13. Favorite Recipes

While you have all that help in the kitchen, begin your child's own recipe box. Copy—or later help your child copy—favorite recipes, and put them in a file box that he has picked out. It never hurts to have another cook in the family—and what a fun, practical keepsake for your son or daughter to take along to his or her first apartment.

14. Telling and Writing

When you have a little more time, ask your child to tell you a story about the picture she's drawn. Write the story as it is told. When your child is older, encourage her to write all or part of it. Fold up the story and picture, put them in an envelope, and send them to a favorite grandparent or other relative. There's no reason anyone in the family should have a bare refrigerator door.

15. Grocery Lists

Let your child help with the grocery list. You could even offer to buy one or two items if he can write them on the list himself. You might try having the child copy down the brand name of an item that you need. At the store, your child can look for that item, matching the word on the list to the name on the item.

16. Chore Time

Have your child make out a chart listing the chores he can help with around the house. Leave room for stars or stickers when the chores are completed. An extra good helper might deserve a special treat.

17. Handmade Cards

Don't let greeting card companies have all the fun! Make handmade cards a tradition at your house. Everyone enjoys making and receiving a card with a little heart in it and some fingerprints on it.

18. Magnetic Letters

Get a set of inexpensive magnetic plastic letters that will stick to the refrigerator. Place them within your child's easy reach. When you're busy in the kitchen, these letters will keep him happily—and constructively— occupied. Be prepared, though, to answer lots of "What does this spell?" questions. Take a moment occasionally to spell out words for your child or to help him find the right letters to spell a word that he wants.

19. Little Gifts

Stationery, pens, and pencils are fun and interesting items for your child, and they make excellent gifts. For a young child, include stamped, addressed envelopes to friends and relatives to make sure that those special letters get sent. A rubber stamp with her name and address on it would make an inexpensive and unique birthday gift for a budding correspondent.

20. Special Places

Make sure that your child's room is equipped with easily accessible bookshelves and a good reading light beside the bed. Stock the shelves with his favorite books, along with some that you hope he will eventually want to read.

21. Hidden Treasures

Play the Hidden Treasure Game with your child. Write out a set of clues that you can help your child read, then hide them around the house or yard. The first clue should lead to the second clue and so on, until your child finally reaches the hidden treasure. This may be anything from a small treat to an Easter basket to a special birthday present.

22. Puppet Shows

Many of us have warm memories of paper-bag puppets from our own childhood. These are not only fun for your child to make, but they also lead naturally to your child's writing a play for the puppets to star in. You might

want to write the play together, talking over ideas for characters and plots (Who does what next?). You and your child can perform the play at a party or family gathering.

23. Fun with Chalk

Put a chalkboard within your young child's easy reach in an area where you spend a lot of time (at-home office, basement workbench, kitchen, family room). Children love to practice writing letters and words—especially their own names. A strategically placed chalkboard can keep your child constructively busy while you work on your own project.

24. Time Capsule

Have your child collect some of his writings and drawings and put them in a box he has decorated. This box can be used as a time capsule, with the child sealing it and putting the date it is to be opened on the outside. You might also write a letter to your child in the future; place it in an envelope with the instruction that it not be opened until your child's tenth or sixteenth birthday.

25. Books Galore

Make room for your child's books and magazines in the family or living room. You can make it as convenient for her to pick up a good book as it is for her to turn on the television.

Make bedtime more pleasant with a favorite book.

Share bedtime prayers with your child.

At Bedtime

Bedtime can be a special—or an especially difficult—time for you and your child. Experts agree that developing some kind of routine can make bedtime less painful and more pleasurable. In this section we present some ways you can use reading or writing as part of the bedtime routine.

26. Bedtime Stories

The bedtime story is an old idea, but it's a good one. Reading a short book to your child is certainly more pleasant than arguing with her about why she can't stay up "just a little longer." It's fun for both of you when you choose a favorite book from your own childhood and read a chapter or a few pages a night. *Heidi* and *The Black Stallion* are still as good as you remember them to be.

27. Let Him Read

When your child is old enough to read, let him read the bedtime story to you. You might want to take turns reading pages or chapters of a special book. Later on, when he's reading on his own, a good way to encourage more reading is to set bedtime a half-hour earlier than necessary, but say that it's all right to leave the light on and read for a little while.

28. Children as Storytellers

If you're just too tired or too busy to read, then have your child tell you a story. Pick a favorite stuffed animal or doll, and ask your child a leading question or two: "How did this bear get such big eyes?" "Was this bunny ever lost in the woods?" As you listen to a charming story, you will be hearing about your child's own self.

29. Taking Turns

Alternate telling a story from night to night. You start the story one night, with your son adding to it the next night, and so on.

30. Sing-Along

Play one of your child's favorite songs on a record or tape player and sing along with it.

31. Making Memories

Keep a diary together. Take five or ten minutes at the end of each day to talk about and write down important or fun things that happened. A joint diary, kept over the years, will help keep the lines of communication open between you and your child. It will also be an invaluable keepsake of the growing-up years you spent together.

32. Sweet Dreams

Invent a pleasant dream before bedtime. You tell your dream to your child, and he tells you his, or invent dreams for each other.

33. Bedtime Prayer

If you like to "say your prayers" at bedtime, pray with your child. Listen to your child's prayers. Let your child hear your prayers. Take turns praying together, and use your own words or any of the prayers that have blessed many a bedtime:

Now I lay me down to sleep,
I pray Thee, Lord, this child to keep.
Thy love stay with me through the night
Until the morning brings its light.

On the road, take along a small recorder to listen to stories on tape or to make a record of the sights and sounds of your trip.

❧

On the Road

"Are we there yet?"
"I have to go to the bathroom!"
"I'm hungry!"

Repeated at thirty-second intervals, these phrases make up the nerve-wracking chorus of bored children in the car. Word games and reading and writing activities can help change that tune.

34. Rhyme Game

A simple rhyming game is fun and good practice for young children who are learning that certain letters represent certain sounds. A parent supplies the first word: "C-A-R spells car," and then changes the first letter to produce a rhyming word: "T-A-R spells _____." The child figures out—with help, if needed—what the word is. Make the list of rhyming words as long as possible: "F-A-R spells _____," "S-T-A-R spells _____," and so on. (It may be a long trip to where you're going.)

35. Your Own Museum

Most children are natural collectors of things, as you find out by what's in their pockets on wash day. On trips, encourage your child to collect things—rocks, leaves, feathers. Have her write information about the object on a 3" x 5" card: what it is, where and when it was found, what it's used for. When you return home, your child can set up a museum display of the items collected on the trip.

36. Handy Books

Keep a small book or two in the glove compartment. Read to your child, or have her read to you.

37. Cliffhangers

Cliffhangers are a fun way to build a story orally. Someone starts a story, continuing until some exciting spot is reached, then breaks off, leaving the next person to continue. This goes on until the story is resolved—or until the story gets too silly to continue.

38. Travelogue

On a trip, take along a small tape recorder. Record impressions, conversations, and gen-

eral descriptions as you travel. Keep the tape
—or a handwritten or typed manuscript of the
tape—with the photographs from your trip.

39. Spelling Game

For the child who is beginning to read,
play a simple spelling/guessing game. Spell
the names of things that you observe, and let
your child guess what it is you're spelling: "I
see a C-O-W." Give as many hints as she
needs.

40. Looking Ahead

For longer trips, go to the library ahead of
time and pick out books related to your destination, as well as to the places through which
you will be traveling. Include some books with
interesting pictures. As you travel, you and
your child can browse through the books, look
up answers to questions you both may have
about the places you are passing, and get
ready for what's coming next.

41. Signs

On short, familiar trips, point out and read
any signs you pass. Whenever you make the
same trip, play a game to see how many signs
your child can remember or point out or read.

42. Matching Game

Let your child fashion a set of picture cards using crayons, old magazines, glue, and 4" x 6" note cards. When she's finished, you print the names of the pictures on another set of 4" x 6" cards. Put them, along with a handful of paper clips, in a small resealable bag and keep them in the glove compartment. They'll be good for any number of games to keep hands busy and the mind active, matching words to pictures.

43. "A" Is for Alliteration

A simple game of alliteration can be fun for toddlers. Choose a letter of the alphabet and take turns naming things that begin with that sound: "M is for monkey," "M is for mommy," "M is for milk," and M is for much more.

44. Portable Felt Board

A folding felt board makes a convenient and inexpensive travel toy. Cut the split bottom from a cardboard box and tape the two pieces together. (This allows the board to fold.) Glue on a piece of felt to cover one side. Then cut out felt letters in various colors. The letters will naturally stick to the board. Keep the letters in a resealable bag for take-along convenience.

45. Memory Game

Another alphabet/memory game can be played with slightly older children. Name your destination and tell one thing that you're going to buy or see when you get there. Begin with something that starts with "A," and take turns adding things to the list, continuing through the alphabet. On each turn, name everything that has been listed previously: "I'm going to the store, and I'm going to buy apples." "I'm going to the store, and I'm going to buy apples and butter." See how long you can make your list.

46. How People Talk

You and your child can tune your ears to the "funny" way people talk in other parts of the country. Share your observations about the differences of language and accent and about the interesting and unusual words you hear people using. Discussing these with your child will make you both more aware of language.

Help your child use the yellow pages to
select a good place to eat.

At the grocery store, have your child
read you the shopping list.

❧

Out and About

More and more, parents are taking their children with them—running errands, going out to eat, attending plays and concerts. Whether your child is sitting beside you because you thought he'd enjoy the music or because you couldn't find a sitter, reading and writing activities can make these times more fun and more worthwhile.

47. "I Gotta Go. . . ."

A simple first reading experience for many children is learning to read the signs on the restroom doors—very important information! Look for the proud smile when your child can tell the difference between "MEN" and "WOMEN."

48. Programs and Bulletins

Make sure that your child gets a program for the play or concert you're about to hear or see. Reading to or with him will help make that time before the show less fidgety. It will also help him enjoy the show more once it starts. In church, you might try reading parts of the bulletin or the hymnal quietly with your child. Some churches have special bulletins for children.

49. Going out to Eat

If you're going out to eat, let your child help pick out the restaurant. Look together through the yellow pages or newspaper advertisements to help make the choice.

50. Reading the Menu

At a restaurant, make sure that your child gets a menu. Encourage her to order for herself, pointing out and reading items she might be interested in. Eventually, she will identify familiar items on the menu herself and will try to figure out unfamiliar ones.

51. Always Have a Crayon

Be sure to keep pens, pencils, and a crayon or two in your glove compartment or purse. A paper placemat in a restaurant makes a great drawing and writing surface.

52. Little Shoppers

At the grocery store, let your child read the list of items you need. Give him a pencil so he can cross out items as you put them into the cart.

53. Reading Ingredients

There are some things you want your child to eat, and some things you don't. Help him learn to recognize certain watchwords on products' labels. He might still want that box of cereal with the cartoon character on the front, but if he sees that sugar is the first ingredient listed, he will have at least some idea why it's better not to eat it.

54. At the Gas Station

At the gas station, you can help your child read the signs and prices, the different kinds and grades of gas, and the brand names of cars and trucks.

55. Recognizing Labels

Let your toddler see if he can pick out the brand-name items that you buy regularly. Read any labels he thinks might be the right ones. When he picks out the right label, read that label two or three times with him. Next time you're in the store, let him try again. Soon he will be able to recognize the label by name as well as by color and design.

56. At the Movies

Movie theaters are full of signs. Your toddler will enjoy the sense of independence he gets from learning how to read "Popcorn," "Restrooms," and "Telephone." With your help, he might even be able to figure out which doors in a multiplex cinema to go through for the movie you want.

57. Who's in the Show?

As adults, we automatically scan titles and credits as they roll up the screen. Take the time to whisper them to your child. Even very young children like to know why all those words are on the screen.

58. Waiting in Line

There's nothing like waiting in line to make a child unhappy. While you're waiting together to pay for your groceries, buy your movie tickets, or see Santa Claus, another little alphabet game can make the time go faster. Look around you at candy-bar wrappers, magazine covers, people's t-shirts—wherever there are letters. Try to find, in order, all the letters of the alphabet. If your child is young, you'll probably want to look together. Older children might enjoy making it a contest.

59. Running Errands

When you have to run errands around town and are taking your child with you, explain to her the names of the places you are going and the directions for getting there. Then as you drive to each place, have her try to draw a map of the trip, including writing down the street names and the various places you stop. She can watch for street signs and copy the names from signs when you arrive at each point along your journey.

60. At the Library

Long before your child can read, he is ready for his first library card. Most libraries have special children's sections where he can pick out books for you to read to him or books he just wants to look at on his own. A trip to the library can make a nice outing for your child and his sitter, as well. The sooner your child gets a library card, the more likely he will be to make books and libraries natural and important parts of his life.

If the library rules allow, don't take home a mere four or six books; bring them home by the bag. Let there be books aplenty!

While you're away from your child, you can each write
stories to share when you're together again.

When You're Away

It is a fact of contemporary life that many parents have to travel as part of their jobs. This travel, however, can be turned to your child's advantage with only a little bit of effort on your part. In this section, we present ideas for activities that can include you in your child's life while you're away from home. These activities also help your child grow in his ability to read and write.

61. Bedtime Message

Before you leave on a trip, jot a special message to your child and slip it under the pillow on her bed. Your child will look forward to receiving the message, and you will have established a link with her to compensate for being away from home.

62. Hearing Your Voice

Spend a few minutes with a tape recorder before you leave on a trip. Either read a story—perhaps one of your child's favorites or one you've been reading to her in person—or leave your own message for her to play back while you are away. Tell her about where you are going and what you are doing. Tell her when you will return. If you are to be gone for several days, she can mark the calendar— and don't forget to call.

63. Answering Questions

Before you leave on a trip, have your child write down—or dictate to you—a couple of questions concerning your destination. The child may want to know what the ocean looks like in San Francisco or how big the Statue of Liberty is. Take a minute during your trip to get the answers, jot them down, and share the information when you return home.

64. Pictures from a Trip

If your child is too young to read or write, sketch major attractions that you see, or collect pictures from airline and hotel magazines and travel brochures. Then either label the pictures or print a short descriptive sentence. Perhaps your child will want to sketch and label things she sees while you are away.

65. Mementos

Bring home interesting brochures, maps, menus, placemats, and other information trinkets you pick up on your travels. Since "it's the thought that counts," this thoughtful kind of coming-home gift is far more valuable than an overpriced stuffed animal bought at the last minute in an airport shop.

66. A Secret Message

Before you leave, ask your child to draw or write a message to you and seal it in an envelope so you can open it and read the message when you reach your destination.

67. Newspapers

You might also bring home cartoons from a distant newspaper or an article about sports or some other topic in which your child is interested. Have your child keep an eye out for articles in the local paper at home in which you might be interested. Share these when you return.

68. Send a Card

Be sure to carry stamps with you on trips so you can pick up post cards and mail short notes home. It takes only a minute, and even if your return beats the delivery, the card is a way of sharing your trip with your child.

69. Get a Card

You might also preaddress and stamp envelopes or cards to the hotel where you will be staying on a long trip. This will make it easy for your child to drop you a letter while you're out of town.

70. Thinking of You

Before you leave on a trip, agree to set aside ten minutes when you, at your end, and your child, at home, will sit quietly and think about each other. Write down what you'd say if the two of you were together.

71. Two Tales

Before you leave on a trip, plan to invent a story with your child, each of you making up a story on the same theme, for example, "The Day I Met the Giant Banana." Any silly idea will work. When you return, share each other's stories and compare how alike and different they are.

72. Sports Talk

If you and your daughter share an interest such as following a local sports team, ask her to keep a record of how the team does while you are away. She becomes a sports journalist. Perhaps you can do the same about a team on the other side of the country.

73. Telegram

Instead of always phoning home, send a telegram. It's another way of reaching out to your family, and it shows that you value the printed word as a means of communication.

74. Special Time

When you return from a long trip, spend some special time with your child. Perhaps the two of you could take a walk together. The important thing is to talk, to listen, to share. Make this a homecoming routine. Children look forward to it, and it helps both of you catch up on each other's activities.

Read the television program guide with your
children to select family viewing.

Encourage your child to write a fan letter
to her favorite TV star.

Using Television

Many people think that television is the cause of most of the problems our children have with reading and writing. Without going into all the pros and cons, we assume that most homes have television and that children will watch it regularly. How, then, can you use television for your child's benefit? Use it as a tool to help your child learn to read and write.

75. What Happens Next?

When you are watching a dramatic television show together, and a commercial comes on, each family member could write down what he or she thinks will happen next in the plot of the story. The key is getting everyone to write something down. The person who comes closest might win some kind of prize— such as having the losers go pop the popcorn.

76. Your Own Show

Most young television viewers are familiar with the typical sitcom format. Have your family imagine that television producers want to make a sitcom based on your family's life. They've asked you to come up with the basic idea for the show and a first script. Work together to write the script.

77. Sell Your Sibling

Draw family names out of a hat. Each family member writes a commercial to "sell" the good aspects of the person whose name was drawn.

78. Play-by-Play

If your child is interested in sports, turn the sound down on a broadcast and take turns being the announcer. This activity will help develop skills in both observing and speaking.

79. Comic Books

If your child likes TV cartoons, don't be afraid to buy the comic books that are packaged and marketed to go along with cartoons. Many good readers have started out by reading supermarket comics.

80. Young Cartoonists

You might also have your child write and illustrate her own comic book. She can start with familiar TV characters and then develop her own. As with other book ideas, this comic book could be duplicated cheaply and distributed to playmates, friends, and relatives.

81. Choosing a Show

Instead of allowing your child to channel-surf, read through the television program guide with him. Talk about various shows and which ones might be interesting to watch. Get your child in the habit of reading about the program first and being selective in what shows he watches.

82. Fan Mail

You and your child can each write a fan letter to your favorite television personality. Most media personalities, from Hollywood stars to politicians, have someone who answers their mail, so you're almost guaranteed some kind of response; once in a while, you may even get a personal note.

83. The Family News

Watch the news shows together. Then, for a family gathering, write and perform your own version of "The Family News," bringing everyone up-to-date on family doings.

84. TV Trivia

Make up your own television trivia game. Use different colored 3" x 5" cards for different categories: sports, cartoons, sitcoms, game shows, soap operas, news. Make up questions over a week or two of television viewing. Then one evening, instead of watching television, make a bowl of popcorn and have your own TV Trivia Contest.

85. Understanding Commercials

Talk about commercials with your child, trying to help her analyze and understand how commercials work—how they get us interested in the product and make us want to buy it. After seeing a commercial, you and she jot down what kind of factual information you received from the commercial message. If there isn't much factual information, talk about what impression the commercial made, how it affected you, and why.

86. What If . . . ?

Play the "What if . . . ?" game with a television show. For instance, take a police show and ask, "What if the hero were a woman instead of a man?" or "What if the villain hadn't escaped at the critical moment?" Playing this game will get your child thinking about such things as plot and other ways the show might have been written. You're helping your child become an active, not a passive, viewer.

87. Multiplying Options

If you are worried that your child is watching too much television, sit down together and come up with a list of things he likes to do in addition to watching television. Select one of these each week and do it in place of watching a television show that you both agree is "not our favorite."

Set aside quiet time for homework every day.

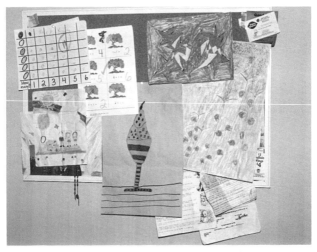

Display your child's pictures and
papers in a place of honor.

❦

Success in School

All of these 101 activities can, in several ways, help your child succeed in school. Specifically, however, the ideas in this section will help you support your child's learning in school with learning in the home. Seeing your child off to school for the first time can make you feel a little helpless. Another adult, the teacher, is going to enter your child's life in a role of gradually increasing importance. How can you be sure that your child is getting a good education and taking advantage of the opportunities presented at school? That the two of you will maintain your close, warm relationship? Here are some reading and writing activities that can help.

88. "How Was School Today?"

Be sure to talk—and listen—to your child about the school day. Don't settle for, "It was okay." Ask specific questions: "What did you do during recess?" "Did you learn any new songs?" With an older child, discuss the new ideas that he is learning and the important events that affect you both. It only takes a few minutes, and it's a language activity that will become a worthwhile habit.

89. School Books

Encourage your child to bring her reading book home. She'll take great delight in reading to you. Be sure to praise her efforts. This will also give her the chance to talk about the stories she reads, discussing favorite characters, possible ways to change the story, and words that are fun or unfamiliar.

90. Time for Homework

Even in the primary grades, your child will probably bring work home occasionally. Set aside a quiet half-hour each day for her to do her work, read a favorite book, draw, or write. It's important to make this time a pleasure, not a punishment.

91. A Place for Homework

Try to include in your child's room a desk or other large, smooth writing surface, a good reading light, paper, pens, pencils, and a few art supplies. Even if he ends up doing most of his homework at the kitchen table, he will probably use this space at least occasionally. Just by being there, it is a sign to him that reading and writing are important.

92. Comparing Notes

At work or at home, if you find yourself thinking about your child, jot down a quick note: "It's 10:30. What are you doing now?" Have your child do the same while he's at school. When you get home, compare questions and see if you can answer them. This can be the basis for a fun discussion and a good way to keep in touch.

93. Work to Be Proud Of

Your child will probably bring home hundreds of papers and pictures during her primary years. Make sure to post some of these on the refrigerator. They can also be hung in the child's bedroom or playroom, or sent to a grandparent. Take time to look at, and comment on, those papers that must be returned to school.

94. Message in a Lunchbox

Children love to get messages from their parents. Slip a message into your child's lunchbox. It can be written in a secret code or backwards, or may be as simple as, "I love you. Have a great day!" It can be anything to indicate to your child that writing is a way for people to communicate their thoughts and feelings, and to show that you value writing. You'll know this activity is worthwhile the day you get to the office, open your briefcase, and find a secret message inside from your child.

95. Visiting School

Take advantage of opportunities to visit your child's school. All schools have parent/teacher conferences, and most have some kind of back-to-school visitation. There might also be an opportunity for you to visit your child's classroom. You could talk to the class about your own occupation or a favorite hobby, or do what you do at home so enjoyably—read a story.

96. From Memory

Memorizing is a worthwhile activity and can be fun as well. Help your child memorize a favorite poem or song; or, with your child, memorize alternate stanzas. With an older child, memorize the Preamble to the Declaration of Independence.

97. Buying Books

Once in a while, your child may bring home an order form from school for paperback books. Make ordering at least a book or two part of your monthly budget. This will strengthen your child's attitude that reading is valuable, and over the years, it will build up quite a library.

98. Books from School

Primary teachers often read a chapter or so a day to their students from a special book. If you can, get a copy of the book and read it yourself. It will be fun and informative for you to discuss the book with your child.

99. Show and Tell

Encourage your child to take a favorite book or story he wrote to school for "Show-and-Tell." Reading and writing are things to be proud of.

100. Sharing Books

When your child begins reading longer books on her own, ask her to recommend a book to you. Not only can you talk about the book together, but you can also begin a new level of sharing. Recommending books to each other is a kind of sharing that grows as your child grows.

101. Invented Spelling

When your child is learning to write, she will want to write lots of words that she doesn't know how to spell. Encourage her to use "invented" spellings rather than interrupt the flow of a story or sentence. An invented spelling is simply spelling a word the way she thinks it might be spelled or sounds like it ought to be spelled. If need be, she can draw a picture to represent the words she cannot spell. Imagination comes first, then improvement. Correction of spelling can come along gently and gradually. With a computer, it comes automatically.

Afterword

Often we think of reading and writing as essential skills that our children must master if they are to be successful in their careers, and certainly this is true. It is also true that our idea of democracy is dependent upon having an educated, informed citizenry. People who can think clearly and inventively, and express themselves effectively have a better chance at remaining free. Reading and writing, speaking and listening are heavy-duty work and a democratic responsibility.

At the same time, we hope that you find in the activities we have shared with you something else that is equally important: Reading and writing are great joys in and of themselves. Helping our children discover this joy is one of the best gifts we can give them.

❦
Resources for Parents

Allison, Christine. *I'll Tell You a Story, I'll Sing You a Song: A Parent's Guide to the Fairy Tales, Fables, Songs, and Rhymes of Childhood*. New York: Dell, 1991.

Clay, Marie. *Writing Begins at Home: Preparing Children for Writing before They Go to School*. Portsmouth, New Hampshire: Heinemann, 1987.

Fox, Barbara J. *Rx for Reading: How the Schools Teach Your Child to Read and How You Can Help*. New York: Penguin Books, 1989.

Freeman, Judy. *Books Kids Will Sit Still For*, 2nd revised ed. New Providence, New Jersey: R. R. Bowker, 1990.

Hauser, Jill Frankel. *Growing up Reading: Learning to Read through Creative Play*. Charlotte, Vermont: Williamson Publishing Company, 1993.

Kaye, Peggy. *Games for Reading: Playful Ways to Help Your Child Read*. New York: Pantheon Books, 1984.

Reed, Arthea J. S. *Comics to Classics: A Parent's Guide to Books for Teens and Preteens*. New York: Viking Penguin, 1994.

Simic, Marjorie R., Melinda McClain, and Michael Shermis, *The Confident Learner: Help Your Child Succeed in School*. Bloomington, Indiana: Grayson Bernard Publishers and the Family Literacy Center, 1992.

Simic, Marjorie R., Melinda McClain, and Michael Shermis, *The Curious Learner: Help Your Child Develop Academic and Creative Skills*. Bloomington, Indiana: Grayson Bernard Publishers and the Family Literacy Center, 1992.

Simic, Marjorie R. and Eleanor Macfarlane. *Family Book Sharing Groups: Start One in Your Neighborhood!* Bloomington, Indiana: Family Literacy Center and EDINFO Press, 1995

Smith, Carl B. with Susan Moke and Marjorie R. Simic. *Connect! How to Get Your Kids to Talk to You.* Bloomington, Indiana: Family Literacy Center and EDINFO Press, 1994.

Smith, Carl B. *Help Your Child Read and Succeed: A Parents' Guide.* Bloomington, Indiana: Grayson Bernard Publishers, 1991.

Trelease, Jim. *The New Read-Aloud Handbook.* 2nd revised ed. New York: Viking Penguin, 1989.

Venson, Sheila. *A Black Parents' Guide to Laying the Foundation for Their Children's Educational Success.* Chicago: Alternative School Network, 1990.